ANIMAL ARCHITECTS

How MAMMALS
Build Their Amazing Homes

W. Wright Robinson

BLACKBIRCH PRESS, INC.

WOODBRIDGE, CONNECTICUT

Acknowledgement

The author thanks Dr. John A. King, Dr. T. L. Yates, Dr. Stephen H. Jenkins, and Dr. Charles A. Long for their help in reviewing all or part of the material for this book.

Dedication

To Ann Lewis Shields. May she always go gently and in peace with a desire to understand all living things.

Published by Blackbirch Press, Inc.
260 Amity Road
Woodbridge, CT 06525

©1999 by Blackbirch Press, Inc.
First Edition

e-mail: staff@blackbirch.com
Web site: www.blackbirch.com

Printed in Hong Kong

10 9 8 7 6 5 4 3 2 1

Library of Congress Cataloging-in-Publication Data

Robinson, W. Wright.
How mammals build their amazing homes/ W. Wright Robinson. — 1st ed.
     p.   cm. — (Animal architects)
     Includes bibliographical references and index.
     Summary: Describes how mammals such as beavers, chimpanzees, moles and badgers build homes to keep them safe from predators and the elements.
     ISBN 1-56711-381-8 (library binding : alk. paper)
     1. Mammals—Habitations Juvenile literature. [1. Mammals-Habitations.
2. Animals—Habitations.]
I. Title. II. Series.
QL706. 2. R625   1999
599.156'4—dc21   99-14385
                                                                   CIP
                                                                    AC

Contents

Introduction

The dictionary describes an architect as "a person whose profession is to design buildings and direct their construction." But people are not the only architects in the world! Human architects are at the end of a long line of remarkable builders. We are actually the most recent builders on the planet. Millions of years before the first human built the first building, animals were building their homes. Some even built large "cities."

Animal architects do not build from drawings or blueprints. Rather, they build from plans that exist only in their brains. Their building plans have been passed from parent to offspring over the course of millions of years.

Meet the Animal Architects

This book will introduce you to just a few of the many fascinating animal architects in the world today. You will discover how they design both resting and living spaces, cradles in which to raise their young, and places to gather and store their food. Most important, you will see how their buildings help them survive in the natural world.

Each group of animals has its own unique methods of construction. Clams, snails, and a few of their relatives build some of the most beautiful structures in all of nature. Their empty homes are the seashells you find at the beach.

Bees, ants, termites, and wasps are among the most interesting architects in the world of insects. They work alone or in large groups to build some remarkably complex homes. Some nests grow larger than a grocery bag and can include five or six stories, with entrances and exits throughout.

Spiders are magnificent architects whose small, often hard-to-find silk homes are every inch as complex and amazing as the larger homes of birds and mammals. Some spiders actually build trapdoors to hide themselves and ambush prey. Others construct beautiful square silken boxes as traps, while they hang suspended in the air!

Birds are another group of remarkable architects. Most people think a bird's nest is simply made of sticks and grass in the shape of a bowl. While this shape describes some nests, it by no means describes them all. Some, like the edible saliva nests of the swiftlets, for example, are quite unusual. In fact, our human ancestors may have learned to weave, sew, and make clay pots from watching winged architects build their nests!

The constructions of mammals are some of the grandest on Earth. Mammals are thinking animals. They can learn from their experiences and mistakes. Each time one of these animals builds a new home, it may be constructed a little differently, a little faster, and a little better.

I hope that you will enjoy reading these books. I also hope that, from them, you will learn to appreciate and respect the incredible builders of the animal world—they are the architects from whom we have learned a great deal about design and construction. They are also the architects who will continue to inspire and enlighten countless generations still to come.

W. Wright Robinson

Meet the Mammals

Most people can recognize a bird or fish, but not everyone is sure which creatures in the animal kingdom are considered mammals. The reason for this confusion could be that mammals look and live very differently from one another. Dogs, cats, horses, bears, tigers, and humans are mammals—but so are whales, porpoises, seals and bats. Mammals live in almost every kind of habitat. There are mammals in the ocean and mammals underground. Some mammals live in trees and others live in deserts.

Even though these animals are very different from one another in many ways, they have two things in common: they all have backbones, and they all feed their young with milk from special glands in the mothers' bodies. These two distinguishing characteristics are shared by all mammals.

Why Mammals Build Homes

Most wild animals live dangerous lives, and only the most fit survive. All mammals—big, small, weak, or strong—must rest and must raise their families. During these times, animals are the most vulnerable (open to danger) and need protection from their enemies.

Mammals have many different ways of getting the protection they need. Horses and cattle, for example, live in herds, where safety is offered by sheer numbers and blending together. Animals, such as raccoons and foxes, often find well-hidden places to live. Other mammals build their own safe homes.

Mammals come in an amazing variety of shapes and sizes.

Types of Mammal Houses

Some mammals, like chimpanzees and squirrels, build their homes above ground. Others, such as badgers, prairie dogs, and moles, live below ground. The European harvest mouse camouflages its home. Still others, like muskrats and beavers, build their homes in and around water. These houses range from simple beds to complex structures that often alter the landscape and environment in significant ways.

FOUR ORDERS OF MAMMALS

An order is a small grouping of animals with similar characteristics. These are the four orders of mammals discussed in this book. For a complete listing of all nineteen orders of living mammals, see the table on page 57.

Order	Description	Number of Species
Insectivora	Insect-eating mammals	400 species, including moles
Primates	Front and hind feet, five toes	165 species, including chimpanzees
Rodentia	Gnawing mammals One pair of chisel-like front teeth in upper jaw and one pair in lower jaw	1,690 species, including beavers, mice, muskrats, squirrels, prairie dogs
Carnivora	Meat-eating mammals	285 species, including badgers with claws and large, sharp teeth

Chimpanzees (Primates)

Mole (Insectivora)

Badger (Carnivora)

Beaver (Rodentia)

Prairie dogs (Rodentia)

Although it is instinct that first helps animals build their homes, many can learn to improve their skills. The mammals that you will meet in this book are thinking animals that often learn from their experiences and mistakes. Each time one of these animals builds a new home, it may be put together a little differently, with improvements for safety, comfort, or durability. Because mammals can learn and apply knowledge, members of the same species may build homes that are similar, but not exactly alike.

CHAPTER

Homes Above Ground

Chimpanzees, gray squirrels, and harvest mice are just three of the many types of mammals that build their houses above ground. They each build their houses for the same reason: to protect themselves and members of their families from enemies. Each of these animals, however, builds a house that is very different in size and structure from the others.

A chimpanzee builds a simple, open nest in high tree branches. This nest keeps a sleeping chimpanzee above the ground where many dangerous predators roam at night. A gray squirrel also builds its nest high above the ground, but this nest has walls and a roof. The inhabitants of this nest are protected from bad weather and from enemies in the sky.

The European harvest mouse builds its home among stalks of tall grasses. Its house is not high above the ground, but because this small mouse is a master of camouflage, it is well hidden. The harvest mouse's home is so hard to see that it keeps its inhabitants quite safe from attack.

Beds in Branches

Although many different kinds of animals live and sleep in trees high above the ground, a chimpanzee actually makes a bed there. This bed, called a nest, allows a chimpanzee to sleep safely and somewhat comfortably.

Chimpanzee nests are sturdy and often very high in the air. Some of these nests can easily support a full-grown human—although there are probably not many people who would like to sleep in a chimpanzee's bed! Chimp nests may be up to 80 feet (4.5 to 24 meters) above the ground—that's the height of an 8-story building!

Chimpanzees are very intelligent animals, so you might think they would build complex nests. This, however, is not the case. A chimpanzee builds its nest in just three simple steps. And the whole construction process takes very little time. From start to finish, a chimp can complete a tree-top nest in less than five minutes.

Making the bed

The first step in building a nest is to find a good place to make a bed. A chimpanzee usually looks for a strong, horizontal branch that is shaped like a Y, or for a vertical fork in the tree that has several branches growing out from the trunk.

Next, a chimpanzee bends together the small branches growing around the Y or fork. As he bends the branches down, he grabs them with his feet and holds them in place. Sometimes, the builder just lays one branch over another to form the nest. At other times, he may weave branches together, making the nest very strong.

The final step is to make the bed soft and comfortable. To do this, a chimpanzee pushes the leaves and twigs around the "bed frame" and down into the nest. Sometimes, he also adds a few handfuls of leaves and twigs to make the nest even more comfortable.

PLAYING HOUSE

Baby chimpanzees spend each night with their mothers in the nest that she has made for them. When these youngsters are just ten months old, however, they may begin to build sleeping nests of their own. Usually, they are just playing when they do this, but each time young chimps try to build a nest, they are learning more about the process. As the years pass, they get better and better at nest-building. By age four or five, chimpanzees have learned how to make their own nests to sleep in at night.

Chimpanzee nests are made from branches, twigs, and leaves and are usually completed in about five minutes.

Sleepless nights

On a dry night, a chimpanzee's open nest is a nice place to sleep. On rainy nights, however, a chimpanzee is miserable—it will most often sit in its nest, head bowed, with its legs pulled close to its chest and its arms wrapped tightly around its body. Chimpanzees dislike rain, but they do nothing to keep it off their beds. They actually have to wait until the rains stop and the nest dries a bit to get a good night's sleep!

Because orangutans build nests that often have roofs, their beds stay dry, even in the rain.

One of the chimpanzee's relatives, however, has found a solution to the rain problem. Orangutans build a type of nest similar to those built by chimpanzees. If it begins to rain, an orangutan climbs up into the branches overhead and builds a second nest, which serves as a roof. After this clever builder has finished the roof, it returns to its bed and goes to sleep, dry and protected from the falling rain.

Leaf Houses

Leaf houses are built by one of the best-known mammals in the eastern region of the United States—the gray squirrel. Although the forest is its natural home, the gray squirrel often builds its nest in the trees of city parks and suburban neighborhoods. This animal's house is known as a dray.

Before construction can begin, a squirrel must first locate a good place to build its home. This step is very important and can determine whether the nest's residents will survive high winds, rain, snow, and hungry predators.

The squirrel usually builds its dray on a large, sturdy tree branch, close to the trunk. The advantage of having the nest there is that the squirrel and its home are protected when strong winds blow. If the nest were built out on a limb, winds could easily destroy it—or could blow another branch into the nest, killing the animals inside. The branch for a squirrel home is usually from 30 to 60 feet (9 to 18 meters) above the ground. With its nest high in the tree, a squirrel is able to escape easily from enemies that cannot fly, and those that are not good climbers.

Squirrel nests, called drays, are made high above the ground with leaves and twigs.

Building the foundation

Construction of a dray usually begins in autumn, when most squirrels prepare for the winter months ahead. A gray squirrel architect begins by building a sturdy foundation for its home. This foundation is made of sticks and twigs that the squirrel gnaws from nearby branches. As more and more of these materials are pushed and woven together, the platform becomes thicker and stronger. The squirrel then adds grasses, leaves, mosses, and bark to give the nest a soft floor that can help to keep the animals warm and comfortable.

Once the foundation is finished, a gray squirrel adds walls and a roof. While holding small sticks and leafy twigs in its teeth or two front feet, the builder weaves and wedges the materials securely into the foundation. The squirrel continues to build the walls higher, slowly curving them inward to form a protective dome roof over the foundation.

Among the leaves and twigs that form the walls and roof, there is a small, well-hidden entrance that leads into the dray. The squirrel builds this entrance to face either the tree trunk or a large nearby limb. This way, the opening of the nest is hidden from enemies and the squirrel can enter or leave its home without being seen.

Winterizing

When the gray squirrel's dray is simply a hollow ball of leaves and twigs, it is about 1 to 2 feet (30 to 60 centimeters) wide. Because the squirrel must prepare its home for the winter, more work needs to be done. The squirrel will not survive the cold weather unless its nest is insulated.

To make its home warmer, the animal lines the inside walls with grasses, leaves, shredded bark, and other soft materials. As the builder packs and weaves these things into place, the walls gradually become thicker. When the dray is finally finished, the squirrel has built a cozy little nest, from 6 to 12 inches (15 to 30 centimeters) wide. Usually, gray squirrels can complete the work on this type of nest in two to five days.

Baby squirrels huddle together, keeping warm inside their den.

DEN DWELLERS

Some gray squirrels live in another kind of home called a den, which is made in the hole of a tree. This hole may be an abandoned woodpecker's nest, or a natural hole where the tree has rotted away. A squirrel lines a den with soft plants to make it cozy and comfortable. Dens that are high above the ground in sturdy old trees are strong and safe, and several generations of gray squirrels may use them for many years.

The outside walls and roof make the dray waterproof, and the thick, well-woven, inside walls allow the nest to retain most of its warmth. Even on very cold days, squirrels can curl up inside the nest and stay warm. During the coldest part of winter, several squirrels may huddle together in the same dray. There, each animal is sheltered by the nest and is warmed by the body heat produced by the other squirrels.

During the winter months, after many trees have lost their leaves, it is easy to see a squirrel's house in the bare branches. The dray may look like a small simple pile of leaves stuck in the treetop, but it is actually a snug, dry place. The squirrel can sleep, hide, and sometimes even raise young in this solid, well-constructed home high above the ground.

Woven Homes

The European harvest mouse is one of the world's smallest mammals. When the animal is fully grown, its body is only about 2 inches (5 centimeters) long and weighs less than 1/3 ounce (10 grams)—about as much as two U.S. nickels.

Harvest mice are found throughout Europe and Asia. They prefer to live in fields of tall grasses where they feed on berries, seeds, grains, and insects. In these grassy fields, the mice build their small, cleverly woven nests. The European harvest mouse is a master builder. It weaves itself a sturdy house out of long grasses and hides it well from the eyes of hungry enemies. Some of their nests are built just for sleeping. Other nests, built as nurseries for newborn mice, are the finest nests made by any harvest mouse. They are not only camouflaged, but padded and comfortable as well.

Preparing the materials

To build her nest, the female harvest mouse climbs up a large stalk of grass and bites the stalk to weaken it. Then she bends the weakened end toward the ground. She may bend a few more nearby stalks in the same way.

The mouse will weave her nest with the leaves that are growing on the bent stalks. First, she tears the long, narrow leaves into thin strips in a very clever way. She holds each leaf with her front feet and bites between two of the veins that run from the stem to the tip of the leaf. Still holding the leaf, she throws her head and shoulders upward, which causes the leaf to tear straight between the veins.

A harvest mouse can build one of nature's best-camouflaged homes among the tall grasses of Europe and Asia.

Leaves are torn and woven together in an intricate way to create a harvest mouse nest.

A harvest mouse may use more than 150 leaves to make her nest. Most of the leaves are broad, with many veins in them, so the builder can sometimes tear one leaf into fifteen or twenty long strips. Because the leaves must remain attached to the stalks, the mouse only splits the top half of each leaf.

Building the nursery

When she has finished making the leaf strips, a female harvest mouse will begin to weave a nest. She weaves the strips around the bent stalks of grass and around one another. Eventually, she forms a bowl-shaped nest. This bowl is the bottom, or floor, of her nursery.

She continues weaving leaf strips to form thick protective walls and a roof around the floor. As the walls grow higher and higher, they gradually curve inward over the bowl to form a dome-shaped roof.

At this point, the nest is a loosely woven grass ball. From inside the nest, she weaves more and more leaf strips into the walls to make the nursery stronger. If there are not enough leaves on the stalks, the little builder nibbles leaves off nearby plants and carries them back to her nest. When the weaving is finally complete, the female harvest mouse has built a sturdy structure that is up to 5 inches (13 centimeters) wide.

Even though the outside of the structure is completely woven, the nursery is not yet finished. To be sure that her babies will have a soft, cozy bed in which to grow, the mother mouse lines the inside of her nest with finely chewed grass and leaves, soft plant parts, and birds' feathers. From start to finish, a nursery can take from two to ten days to build.

Camouflage

The European harvest mouse is very good at building a well-camouflaged nest that can help protect her young. Because the mouse weaves leaves that are still attached to their stalks, the leaves stay alive and green. This way, the nest blends in well with the surrounding plants, making it very hard to see. When the field of grass around the nest begins to die, changing color from green to tan, the nest changes color, too.

Winter homes

During winter, European harvest mice often make their nests in bales of hay, where it is warm. Sometimes, these mice will even move into underground tunnels that were dug by other small animals. When spring returns, however, these little builders once again climb up the tall stalks of grass to weave new homes.

Homes Below Ground

Did you know that some of the first "towns" in the wild west were built by black-tailed prairie dogs? Prairie dogs are just one kind of mammal that likes to build homes underground. The entrance to a prairie dog "city" is surrounded by a mound of soil. This mound gives the inhabitants a lookout post, and also keeps water from flowing into the animals' living area. Prairie dogs build homes with long tunnels, and several connected chambers.

23

The European badger builds long, winding burrows that are often connected in a complex and highly organized way by tunnels and chambers of all kinds. Badger homes have cozy sleeping chambers lined with soft beds of grass. They even have special bathrooms.

The Eastern mole spends almost its entire life underground. It builds a deep burrow, which it uses as its permanent home. This mammal digs shallow runs, as well. These temporary tunnels allow moles to travel from place to place while they are looking for food.

Setts and Cities

Few mammals have homes that are as large or as old as those built by some European badgers. When these animals live in an undisturbed countryside, where food is abundant and the soil is good for tunneling, their burrows may be used for generations. Their intricate underground systems, or networks, are slowly made larger as they are used year after year for decades—sometimes even centuries!

The burrows where badgers live are called setts. They use their homes for sleeping, raising their young, and as protection from danger. European badgers sometimes build small setts for one or two individuals. Other times, they build very large setts, where a group of ten to twelve badgers, called a clan, live and work together.

The tunnels in the sett of a European badger are about 10 inches (25 centimeters) high and 12 inches (30 centimeters) wide. In some places, however, the tunnels are wider so that two badgers can pass by one another if necessary.

Tunneling

Building an underground home is hard work, but badgers are well equipped for the job. Their short, strong, front legs and broad feet with long, sturdy claws do most of the digging. With these tools, a badger can dig through almost any kind of soil.

A European badger tunnels into the ground by scratching at the earth with one front foot and then the other—the action is similar to a dog digging a hole in the ground. The animal loosens the soil with its claws and pushes it back under its body with its front feet. While digging close to the surface, a badger sends most of the loose soil flying behind it in all directions. In this way, a badger can quickly make a hole that is from 1 to 2 feet (30 to 60 centimeters) wide. This hole becomes the entrance to the badger's burrow.

Badgers have broad feet with sturdy claws that enable them to dig easily in almost any kind of soil.

Soon, the animal has dug so deep that it can no longer kick the loose soil to the ground above. To continue, the badger must now work in a different way. As it digs with its powerful front feet, a badger kicks the loose soil back toward the entrance with its hind feet. As it continues to dig, a mound of dirt gradually forms behind the animal.

Before the mound becomes so large that it blocks the entrance, the badger stops digging. Now it works on removing the soil from the tunnel. To do this, the builder backs out of the tunnel until it reaches the mound. Then, while continuing to back out, the animal pushes some of the loose soil toward the entrance with its hind legs. The builder then wraps its front legs around the remaining loose soil, as if hugging the earth, and drags it out of the tunnel and away from the entrance. By digging, kicking, and dragging the unwanted soil, the badger gradually finishes its home.

Temporary setts

One of the simplest setts that badgers build will often be used as a temporary shelter. This shelter is used primarily for protection against the elements or predators. These setts have only one tunnel, often with a bend or curve in it, that leads from the surface of the ground to a room at the far end. This room is called a chamber, and is where the badger sleeps. The builder makes a comfortable bed by covering the floor of the chamber with a thick layer of grasses and leaves that are collected while the animal is above ground.

Badgers are very clean animals. They often have special places in their underground homes that are used as bathrooms.

These places are often referred to as dung pits, or latrines. Even a temporary sett may have a small dung pit.

The temporary sett may seem like a nice home, but it is not as safe as it could be. For example, a dangerous animal could block its single entrance, or rainwater could flow into the tunnel during a severe storm. In either of these situations, the badger would suddenly become trapped in its home.

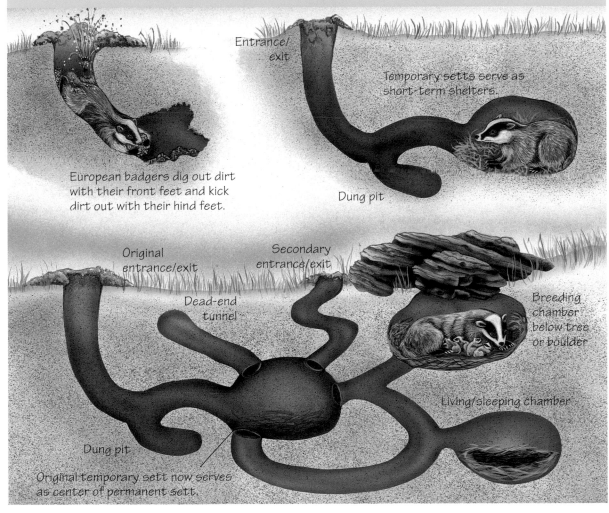

DEVELOPMENT OF A BADGER SETT

European badgers dig out dirt with their front feet and kick dirt out with their hind feet.

Entrance/exit

Temporary setts serve as short-term shelters.

Dung pit

Original entrance/exit

Secondary entrance/exit

Dead-end tunnel

Breeding chamber below tree or boulder

Living/sleeping chamber

Dung pit

Original temporary sett now serves as center of permanent sett.

Permanent homes

Sometimes, a badger converts its temporary sett into a permanent home by adding more tunnels and entrances. To do this, the builder will tunnel through the soil, away from its living chamber, in several different directions. The new tunnels may either come to a dead end, or curve around and connect with another tunnel. Sometimes, a tunnel might slant upward and open to the ground's surface to form another entrance or emergency exit.

When a sett is enlarged in this way, the original living chamber is no longer used for sleeping. Instead, this chamber becomes an important part of the builder's new home—it is where the new tunnels meet. Other living chambers, usually located about 15 to 20 feet (5 to 6 meters) from the nearest entrance, are built throughout the sett. These chambers are between 2 and 3 feet (60 to 90 centimeters) wide and sometimes as much as 2 feet (60 centimeters) high.

Baby badgers' chamber

When it is time for a female badger to give birth, she prepares a breeding chamber where she will feed and raise her young. The breeding chamber is about the same size as a living chamber, but much more carefully constructed.

Badgers usually build breeding chambers just below a boulder, or among the roots of a tree so that the roof is sure to be strong. To make the nurseries even safer, the tunnels leading to these chambers are slanted upward from other tunnels in the sett. These slanted tunnels make it more difficult for the breeding chambers to become flooded by rainwater.

Building additions

A European badger never seems to finish building its home. As the years pass, what may have started as a temporary sett is slowly made larger and larger. Eventually, other badgers, often family members, move into the sett. They, too, begin building tunnels, chambers, and entrances. As generations of badgers continue to work this way, a single underground home becomes enormous. Many setts are thought to be at least 100 years old. One European badger sett in England has been used for more than 400 years!

OUT-OF-SIGHT SETTS

European badger setts are sometimes so large and complex that they are called underground cities. One badger "city" in England had more than 984 feet (300 meters) of tunnels. It also had 18 beds, 12 entrances, and 8 dung pits. To build this sett, the badgers had to carry about 25 tons of soil to the surface of the ground!

Even though the English sett is a large badger home, it is not the largest. Setts with more than 80 entrances have been found. One had almost 2,000 feet (590 meters) of tunnels. These large setts are often built on three or four different levels. They may have tunnels and chambers that are more than 15 feet (4.5 meters) below ground.

It is almost impossible to know the exact size and shape of most of the world's largest setts. There may be even larger, more amazing setts waiting to be discovered in years to come!

Frontier Towns

Some of the earliest-known black-tailed prairie-dog towns were huge. One prairie-dog town found in Texas during the early 1900s was about 250 miles (403 kilometers) long and 100 miles (161 kilometers) wide! It had a population of about 400 million prairie dogs—at that time, fewer than 80 million people were living in the entire United States!

A prairie-dog town is simply a separate and distinct community of prairie dogs. These communities are called colonies. Within a colony, each adult prairie dog lives alone in an underground burrow of its own.

It is hard to tell, from the few mounds that can be seen above ground, that some prairie-dog towns are hundreds of miles long underground.

The burrows of black-tailed prairie dogs are so well built that that they can last for hundreds of years. Unfortunately, most of these animals and their amazing homes were destroyed by ranchers and developers as the frontier was being settled in the 1800s. A few small dog towns, however, can still be found throughout America's West.

Building the burrow

To build its home, a prairie dog uses the five, long, sharp claws at the ends of both front feet. These are the only tools that the builder needs. A prairie dog begins building its burrow by digging a small entrance hole in the ground. This hole is about 6 to 8 inches (15 to 20 centimeters) wide. Just below the entrance, however, the tunnel narrows to only 4 to 5 inches (10 to 13 centimeters) across.

Like badgers, a prairie dog digs with its front feet and kicks the loose soil out of the tunnel with its hind feet. As it builds, the architect slants the tunnel downward, gradually digging deeper and deeper into the ground. Soon, the animal is working so far from the entrance that it can no longer kick the loose soil out of the tunnel. To remove it, a prairie dog may push the soil to the surface with its forehead and front legs. Sometimes, it kicks the soil toward the entrance with its hind legs while backing out of the tunnel.

The length of this narrow, slanting tunnel depends a great deal upon the builder. Prairie-dog burrows range from 20 feet (6 meters) to more than 100 feet (30 meters) long, but the average burrow of a black-tailed prairie dog is about 40 feet (12 meters) in length.

Adding on rooms

Near the end of the burrow, far from the entrance, a prairie dog will build several rooms, or chambers, in its home. Among those chambers are one or two bedrooms, or nest chambers. A nest chamber is most often egg-shaped, about 1.5 feet (46 centimeters) long, and 1 foot (30 centimeters) high. Here, the animal makes a snug, warm bed by lining the floor and walls with a thick mat of dry grasses. A prairie dog will usually build its nest chambers along the main tunnel, about 10 to 15 feet (3 to 4.5 meters) below the surface of the ground. The soil at that depth does not freeze during the winter and helps protect the nest from the cold temperatures above ground.

Prairie dogs line their nest chambers with a thick mat of soft, dry grasses.

Prairie dogs will also build an emergency chamber above the main tunnel, where they can be safe in case of flooding from severe rains. A prairie dog may avoid drowning by climbing into this chamber and waiting there for the water in the tunnel to soak into the ground.

Also, like badgers, some prairie-dog burrows have certain areas that are used as bathrooms. These sections are usually located just off the main tunnel, at the end of a short, dead-end tunnel. Some prairie dogs may also build a separate chamber for this purpose.

The back door

A black-tailed prairie dog has several enemies that are small enough to enter the narrow tunnels of its home. Unfortunately, two of its most dangerous enemies—rattlesnakes and ferrets—can easily hunt within these tunnels. Because of this danger, most prairie-dog burrows have a second opening. This way, the inhabitants have a better chance of escaping, and do not become trapped in their own homes.

The second entrance, or back door, is built off the main tunnel. The builder begins digging a narrow tunnel, called a plunge shaft, that extends almost straight up to the surface of the ground. It is only 4 to 5 inches (10 to 13 centimeters) wide, but it may be as much as 15 to 20 feet (4.5 to 6 meters) long.

Some prairie dogs build a 1-foot-wide (30 centimeter) side chamber along the plunge shaft. The side chamber is usually 3 to 4 feet (0.9 to 1.2 meters) below the ground and is called a turning bay. It gives the prairie dog a place to turn around while it is traveling in the long, narrow passageway.

Entrance mounds

Prairie dogs make good use of the soil that they dig out of the ground. Often, they will scrape the loosened soil into a pile around the entrance hole and use their blunt noses to pack the soil firmly in place. As they dig deeper into the burrow, more soil is added to the pile and packed down. Eventually, the burrow's entrance hole is surrounded by a dome-shaped mound of dirt that may be as much 3 feet (1 meter) high, and more than 10 feet (3 meters) wide.

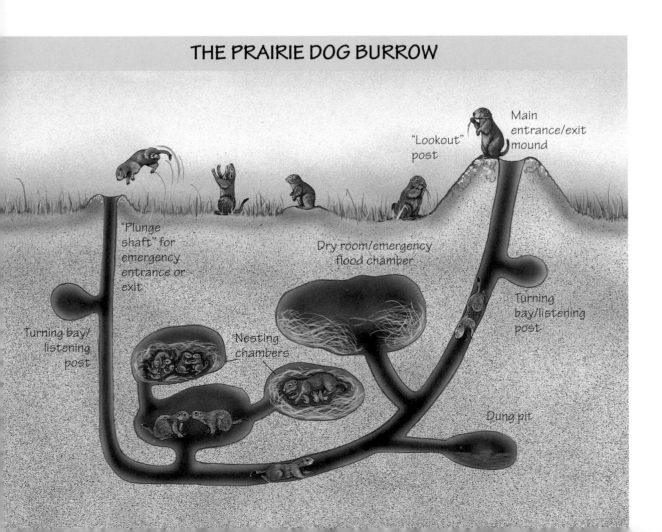

THE PRAIRIE DOG BURROW

"Lookout" post

Main entrance/exit mound

"Plunge shaft" for emergency entrance or exit

Dry room/emergency flood chamber

Turning bay/listening post

Turning bay/listening post

Nesting chambers

Dung pit

Prairie dogs take great care to construct underground homes that stay warm and dry, and offer safety from predators.

The large mound of soil is helpful to a prairie dog in two important ways. The mound keeps water from rushing into the burrow's entrance after a heavy rain. The mound also makes a good lookout post, where a prairie dog can stand and easily see across the flat prairie. If a dangerous animal approaches, the prairie dog can quickly disappear into its burrow.

The second entrance, leading into the plunge shaft, is also surrounded by a mound of soil. This mound, however, is built with soil that the prairie dog pushes into a pile from the surface of the ground around the hole. When finished, it has steep sides and looks like a small volcano.

Hills and Tunnels

Only a few mammals spend most of their lives underground. Of those that do, moles are among the most interesting. They not only sleep and raise their young in their underground nests, they hunt for food in their long tunnels as well.

An Eastern mole prefers to make its home under woodlands or grassy fields, where the soil is often loosely packed and a little moist. In this type of soil, the animal can easily dig a tunnel and disappear into it in only a few seconds. To burrow this quickly, a mole uses its two front feet, which are designed especially for digging. Its legs are short and strong, and they stick straight out from the sides of the animal's body. Its large, flat, shovel-like feet are equipped with powerful claws.

"Swimming" through soil

When a mole begins to dig, it reaches forward with both front feet and then pulls them apart and back to its sides. With this movement, moles can create a small hole in the ground. A tunneling mole then moves forward, puts its snout into the hole, and again uses its feet to make the hole a little deeper. As the digging is quickly repeated, the mole seems to "swim" down through the soil—in a way that looks similar to a person doing the breaststroke in water. Within only a few minutes, a mole can dig its way completely underground.

If the soil is loose enough, a mole may continue using the "breaststroke" to make tunnels just a few inches below the ground's surface. As the animal "swims" through the earth in search of food, some of the soil along the sides of the tunnel is pressed into the walls. The surface of the ground is pushed upward as the animal passes underneath. The roof of a mole's shallow tunnel is very often visible as a long, low ridge that runs along the ground's surface.

These shallow surface tunnels are called runs. During the warmer months, moles travel through them to hunt earthworms, spiders, and insects that live in the topsoil. Moles will hunt only in those runs where food is abundant; they usually do not return to runs where food was scarce.

A mole's shovel-like front legs stick straight out from its sides and are ideal for digging through soil.

Mining sideways

Sometimes, moles must tunnel through soil that is tightly packed. To dig through this type of soil, a mole will dig with one front foot at a time. It braces its other front foot firmly against the floor of the tunnel. At the same time, the animal will push both hind feet against the tunnel walls to gain even more support.

Braced and ready to dig, a mole rotates its body to one side so that its digging foot is on the ceiling of the tunnel. It then pushes this powerful foot upward and back several times very quickly. The animal then turns its body to the other side, so that the other front foot can now dig and push at the soil. Working in this way, the mole slowly moves forward, building its tunnel just below the ground's surface. The roof of this kind of run also appears as a long, low ridge above ground.

BUILDERS WITH BIG APPETITES

The length of a mole's tunnel network may depend on the amount of food in the soil. Moles have enormous appetites and can eat the equivalent of their own weight in food each day. A mole that lives in soil where food is abundant may have a home with only 300 to 400 feet (90 to 120 meters) of tunnels. Moles that lives in soil where food is scarce, however, may need 2,000 to 3,000 feet (609 to 914 meters) of tunnels in which to hunt .

Building the burrow

Runs are just part of the Eastern mole's underground home. About 2 feet (60 centimeters) below these runs, moles dig deep, permanent burrows. There, they are much safer from the dangers above. In the safety of these burrows, a mole builds a nest that is used all year round.

Deep burrows and nests are more difficult to build than the runs. Much of the soil that is loosened as the animal digs must be removed from the burrow. As the animal makes its burrow, it digs with one front foot and braces itself with the other. With its hind feet, it kicks the loosened soil along the floor of the tunnel. Every now and then, the mole turns around and—like a little bulldozer—pushes the loose soil out of the burrow. To do this, the animal walks on three legs and shoves the soil with one of its large front feet. The dirt is pushed along the floor of the burrow and up the nearest vertical tunnel.

THE UNDERGROUND WORLD OF THE MOLE

Shallow runs are used for hunting food.

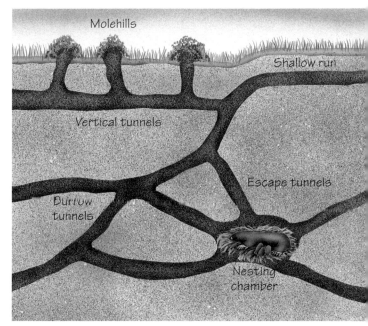

Molehills

Shallow run

Vertical tunnels

Burrow tunnels

Escape tunnels

Nesting chamber

To push out of a burrow, the mole walks on three legs while shoving with one foot.

Making molehills

Moles do not push the soil completely out of their tunnels, however. Instead, they block and hide the tunnel's entrance with the loose soil. This small pile of dirt is called a molehill. As a mole pushes more and more soil to the surface, the molehill gradually becomes larger.

As the animal makes its deep burrows longer, it builds more vertical tunnels close to where it is working. As the builder enlarges its home, it removes more dirt from the new burrows. The animal then makes more molehills at the tops of these tunnels.

Building the nest

Somewhere along one of the deep burrows, a mole will build at least one nest. To do this, it enlarges a small section of the burrow so that it becomes a comfortable chamber about 6 inches (15 centimeters) wide. The builder also digs several more tunnels leading from the chamber in different directions. The mole does this extra work to prevent it from being trapped in a single, dead-end tunnel. To make a soft, cozy place to rest and sleep, a mole gathers dry leaves and grass from above ground and lines the nest with the material.

A mole spends the cold, winter months living and hunting deep within the tightly packed dirt of its burrow. There, the animal feeds on earthworms and other creatures that have moved down into warmer soil. When spring comes and the surface of the ground becomes warmer, the mole returns to the looser topsoil. There, the animal rebuilds its runs and once again hunts for food closer to the surface.

Homes In and Around Water

Muskrats and American beavers are two mammals that build their homes in or around water. Even though they often dig burrows into muddy banks, they also build island homes, known as lodges. A muskrat builds its house with grasses. A beaver uses branches and small logs for its lodge. Both of these clever mammals live safely in their island homes, far away from their enemies, which most often hunt on land.

Making an Island

A muskrat begins building its house during late summer or early autumn. To get started, the builder collects pieces of vegetation from in and around the marsh, swamp, or pond where it lives. The muskrat mixes the vegetation with mud, which helps hold the pieces together. Then, the animal piles the mixture in water about 2 feet (0.6 meters) deep.

As a muskrat adds more mud and plants, the pile slowly gets larger and sinks deeper into the water. Eventually, it will rest firmly on the bottom, and a small, dome-shaped mound of plants will rise up out of the water. The muskrat continues adding plants and mud until the top of the mound is 2 to 5 feet (0.6 to 1.5 meters) above the water's surface.

Next, a muskrat architect makes a tunnel in the mound. It dives underwater to the bottom of the pile. Then, it pushes and chews its way up into the middle of the pile. If a stalk gets in the way, the muskrat cuts it with its sharp teeth, or grabs it with its front feet and moves it out of the way.

Once the tunnel is above the surface of the water, a muskrat will continue pushing the plants aside to hollow out a living chamber inside the mound. The finished chamber is 1 foot (30 centimeters) or more in width, and high enough for the builder to move around easily. A muskrat may then add one or two more tunnels leading into the cozy, little room.

Safety and Shelter

With all of its tunnels, the muskrat's island home is a safe place for this animal to sleep and to raise its young. Because its lodge is usually built in a marsh or swamp, a muskrat is safe from

A muskrat builds its home by gathering plants and branches from around a watery area and mixing these materials with mud.

attack by most land animals. In addition, all of the entrances to the living chamber open underwater, so it is hard for enemies that swim only on the surface, such as otters or minks, to find their way into the muskrat's house. If, however, a dangerous animal does happen to get inside, the inhabitants can escape quickly through one of the other tunnels.

A muskrat's island home provides shelter during the bitter-cold winters in places such as Alaska and northern Canada. The mound walls around the living chamber are often 1 foot (30 centimeters) thick or more. They help to keep the cold air out of the living chamber while they help to retain the heat that is produced by the animal's warm body.

Edible Houses

A muskrat's home can also be a source of food, if necessary. When food is scarce, the animal can eat the plants in the walls of the mound. It cannot eat the walls of its house for very long, however, or soon it would have no house left!

Even when winter temperatures freeze the surface of the water around its home, a muskrat must leave its house to search for food in the water. This search can sometimes take a muskrat far from home. With ice on the surface, however, there is often no place to get a breath of air—and without air the animal could easily drown before it is able to return home. So, in order to survive long, cold winters, a muskrat living in northern regions will build special feeding stations around its home.

A simple feeding station may be a small raft of vegetation that floats on the water and is kept in place by the rooted marsh plants around it. After the surface of the water has frozen, the muskrat can swim under one of these rafts and push its head up through the plants to breathe. The animal can even climb out of the water and onto the ice to eat. This type of feeding station is very dangerous, however, because it does not keep the muskrat hidden from its enemies. Owls, hawks, and other birds of prey can quickly fly down, pick the animal up off of the ice, and bring a muskrat home for dinner.

A large pile of vegetation, which looks similar to the muskrat's house, makes a much safer feeding station. Here, the animal is able to crawl up inside of the mound without being seen. Once inside, a muskrat can rest, get some air before swimming on, or—if hungry—can eat the vegetation in the walls of the station itself.

Push-ups

In places where winters are extremely cold, clever muskrats often build feeding stations called push-ups. Work on the push-up station begins soon after a thin layer of ice covers the water. First, a muskrat gnaws a hole through a weak spot in the ice and piles plants over the hole. Then, the builder crawls up under the plants and pushes them aside and around the hole, digging out a small room under the pile. This dome of wet plants soon freezes in place over the hole.

The push-up does two very important things. First, it gives a muskrat a safe place to hide while away from its lodge. Second, the dome also keeps cold air away from the hole in the ice. Because it is kept warm, the water in the hole does not freeze quickly and does not trap the animal below the ice.

Muskrats are masters at building mounds and domes of vegetation that serve many functions in the water.

MUSKRAT BURROWS

Not all muskrats live in marshes, swamps, and ponds. Some live near slow-moving rivers and streams, where it would be difficult or even impossible to build a dome-shaped grass house. These animals often live in burrows that they dig into muddy banks along the edge of the water.

To build its burrow, a muskrat dives under water and tunnels into a muddy river bank. Inside, the builder slants the tunnel upward. It continues digging until it is above the surface of the water. The muskrat then hollows out a room inside the bank, which becomes its home. Some muskrat tunnels are more than 30 feet (10 meters) long.

A muskrat burrow, like a muskrat lodge, has a dry living chamber above water and an entrance under water. Unlike the lodge, however, a burrow usually has a second entrance that is above water, often under the roots of a tree. With these two entrances, the animal can enter or leave its home by land or by water.

Even those muskrats that build island homes usually move into burrows during the warmer months of the year because they are safer. In the spring, melting snow often causes floods that can damage or even destroy the grass lodges.

Dams and Ponds

Architect, engineer, carpenter, mason, woodcutter, swimmer, and lumberjack—all of these words have been used to describe human builders. But beavers are the only other mammals that have earned the right to be given all these titles. Although beavers are best known for the dams they build, these animals also construct lodges, canals, and long, underground tunnels.

Beavers do not usually work alone when building their structures. They live and work in small groups called clans or colonies. A single colony may have as few as two individuals (usually one male and one female) or as many as twelve members (a mother, father, and their offspring). A colony of beavers, working together, can quickly change its habitat to suit its needs. The work usually begins with the construction of a dam across a small stream.

A beaver's dam

The purpose of a dam is to block the flow of water along a stream. When the flow is blocked, the level of the water behind the dam rises, flooding the land nearby. Gradually, as more and more water flows downstream to the dam, a pond forms.

Beaver dams block the flow of a stream and cause the surrounding area to flood.

Flooding is just what beavers want—and need—to happen. These animals are excellent swimmers and have very few enemies that live in water. On land, however, beavers are clumsy and have many enemies. By building a dam and flooding the surrounding area, a beaver colony can change dangerous forestland into a safe pond in which to live.

Finding the site and materials

First, a beaver colony must find a good location for its dam. These animals look for a shallow, slow-moving stream with firm banks. They also look for an area with a plentiful supply of aspen, birch, willow, or other trees that they can use both for food and building materials.

Beavers have sharp, chisel-like front teeth that easily gnaw through the wood of a tree. Some beavers can cut down trees more than 2 feet (60 centimeters) in diameter. Once the tree is lying on the ground, beavers will cut the branches into lengths that a single beaver is able to carry alone. These expert lumberjacks remove all the branches from the fallen tree, leaving only the trunk behind. If a small, young tree is cut down, the whole tree is pulled to the water, where the beavers are safest, and it is cut apart there.

Building the dam

Once a site is found, construction of the dam begins. Members of a colony carry sticks and branches—some with twigs and leaves still attached—to the site. They push the large ends of these branches into the muddy stream bottom. The small, free ends point downstream, in the direction that the water is flowing.

Above and Right: Long, chisel-like teeth are perfect for gnawing wood.

The builders then pile stones, gravel, mud, and sunken logs onto the large ends of these branches to help secure them in place at the bottom of the stream. The animals bring more sticks and branches to the site, pushing them into the stream's bottom or wedging them under the stones and logs. Gradually, as layer after layer of material is added, the dam gets higher, and the flow of water through the dam slows down.

As they work, beavers scoop up mud from the bottom of the stream with their front paws and use it to help plug openings between sticks and branches. Leaves, twigs, grasses, mud, and anything else being washed down the stream also plug the small holes, helping to block the flow of water.

When the dam is solid enough to keep most of the water from passing through, the level of the water behind the dam rises. Soon, the stream flows over its banks and begins flooding the surrounding land. Beavers will continue adding materials to their dam, slowly making it higher and higher. When the water in the flooded area is about 6 to 10 feet (2 to 3 meters) deep, the dam is high enough and the beavers are almost done. In the final step, the builders cover the upstream side of the dam with a thick layer of mud to stop any leaks.

HOLD THAT WATER!

A finished beaver dam is often 6 feet (2 meters) high and about 10 feet (3 meters) wide at the base. The length of a dam varies, depending on the distance between the banks of the stream. Some dams may be only 10 feet (3 meters) long; others are much longer.

One of the longest beaver dams ever recorded was found in New Hampshire. It reached the incredible length of 4,000 feet (1,219 meters). That's longer than 13 football fields, lined up end to end! A dam of this incredible size must have taken several years to build.

While building a dam, beavers will often bring branches with all the twigs and leaves, still attached, to the construction site.

Temporary housing

While a colony's dam is being built, beavers often live in burrows that they dig below ground. These homes are built only along the edge of the water, in high banks made of soil that is good for tunneling.

The entrance to a burrow is always under water. To make the entrance, a beaver will swim down about 3 feet (1 meter). Then, using its feet, it will dig a tunnel into the muddy bank. Once he is in the bank, he digs a tunnel on an upward slant. He will continue digging until he is above water. A beaver's tunnel is usually about 10 to 15 feet (3 to 4.5 meters) long, but some may be more than 30 feet (9 meters) long.

At the end of the tunnel, the animals hollow out a small living chamber, which is often only 3 feet (1 meter) wide and 1 to 2 feet (30 to 60 centimeters) high. In this small chamber, the beavers sleep, raise their young, and hide from enemies.

The burrow is a safe place for a colony to live while they are building their dam and waiting for their pond to form. Sometimes, however, as the dam grows higher and the water behind it rises, their temporary burrow may become flooded. This forces the beavers to dig their way higher into the bank.

Each time beavers move to a higher spot—closer to the surface of the ground—the roof of soil over their living chamber becomes thinner. When the roof is so thin that it is unsafe, these clever builders strengthen it by piling twigs, branches, and small logs on the ground above. If the rising water once again forces the colony to move higher, the animals simply dig, push, and gnaw their way into the materials piled above the burrow. In this way, the home that started as an underground burrow, may become a home above ground, called a bank lodge. This lodge is similar to the one they build in the water.

A bank lodge is a temporary beaver home that is used while a dam is under construction.

The island lodge

When the dam is finished, the beavers may move away from their bank lodge and build a dome-shaped house in their new pond. This house, also called a lodge, is usually surrounded by water so that the beavers can live safely, beyond the reach of their enemies that hunt on land.

Building an island lodge is very similar to building a dam. It is built in autumn as the beaver colony prepares for the cold, winter months ahead. With mud, gravel, rocks, sticks, and brush, the animals first build a sturdy foundation. They gather the materials and push and wedge them into a pile on the bottom of the pond. Slowly, the pile grows larger. After many hours of work, a platform, about 10 to 20 feet (3 to 6 meters) wide, extends from the bottom of the pond to the surface. The beavers continue building until the top of the platform is about 6 inches (15 centimeters) above the surface of the pond. This large, flat, sturdy island is the foundation upon which the beavers build their house.

Next, the builders construct a dome-shaped roof over their island. First, they pile a layer of brush and other light materials on the island. Then, they pile larger branches and small logs on top of this first layer to form the roof. When the heavy, domed roof is finished, it may be more than 6 feet (2 meters) above the surface of the water.

To make a doorway into their house, beavers will dive underwater to the base of the platform. They dig, push, and chew their way up through the large pile of building materials, making a tunnel as they go. They continue tunneling upward until they are just a few inches above the water's surface.

An island lodge rises high above the water and contains a large living chamber.

Then, they dig a second tunnel on the opposite side of the island. The holes in the floor, where the tunnels enter the lodge, are called plunge holes. They are often 1 to 2 feet (45 to 60 centimeters) in diameter.

The last step is to remove the light brush that was piled onto the island platform to help build the roof. The beavers' finished house has one large, living chamber that is above water. This chamber is usually about 6 to 8 feet (1.8 to 2.4 meters) wide, but only 1 to 2 feet (30-60 centimeters) high. Each member of the colony makes a soft bed, along the walls of the lodge, out of wood that that animal has shredded with its teeth.

Beavers keep their living chamber dry by lining the floor with shredded sticks and bark. This allows the water they bring in to quickly run down through the floor materials and away from the nest. They also slant the floor gently downward, toward the plunge holes, so that water will quickly drain out of the house.

This island home is large and sturdy, and takes at least one month for a beaver colony to build. When the lodge is finished, however, it can be used for many years. One lodge in Russia, for example, was used by generations of beavers for more than forty years.

Ponds and meadows

As clever as beavers are, they cannot build a pond that will last forever. The same streams that carry water also carry soil. Over the years, this soil slowly builds up on the bottom of the pond, and the water becomes more and more shallow. Eventually, the

FOOD CANALS

Beavers are clumsy on land. When they need food, they first cut down only those trees that are growing closest to the edge of the pond. They will, however, eventually need more food. To get it, they dig canals that extend in all directions from their pond into the forest, where trees are plentiful. The beavers cut the trees into easy-to-handle pieces and float them through the canals back to the pond.

Beaver canals are usually 2 to 3 feet (60 to 90 centimeters) wide and up to 3 feet deep. These canals are dug by removing soil handful by tiny handful. Over time, as more trees are needed, a canal may be extended to a length of more than 600 feet (183 meters).

Beavers spend a good deal of time either building new structures or repairing existing ones, which can last for many years.

water is too shallow for the beavers to live in the pond safely. At this point, they must leave their home to build a new dam and make a new pond somewhere else.

The old pond slowly disappears as the dam rots away. Grasses begin to grow in the rich soil that was once on the bottom of the pond. Soon, all that is left of the water is a stream, flowing through the grassy meadow that was once home to generations of hard-working mammal engineers and expert pondmakers.

Classification Chart of Mammals

Within the animal kingdom, all animals with similar character-istics are separated into a smaller group called a phylum. Similar animals within a phylum are separated into a smaller group called a subphylum. Animals within a subphylum that are most similar to one another are then separated into several smaller groups: class, order, family, genus, and species.

The following table provides information about the phylum, subphylum, class, and nineteen orders of living mammals. Members of the four orders of mammals that appear in bold type are discussed in this book.

Classification
KINGDOM: Animalia
PHYLUM: Chordata
SUBPHYLUM: Vertebrata
CLASS: Mammalia

Order	General Description	Examples	Approximate Number of Species
Monotremata	Egg-laying mammals	Duck-billed platypuses, echidnas	6
Marsupialia	Pouched mammals	Opossums, kangaroos, koalas	240
Insectivora	Insect-eating mammals	Moles, shrews	400
Dermoptera	Gliding mammals	Flying lemurs	2
Chiroptera	Flying mammals	Bats	875
Primates	Mammals whose front and hind feet have five toes	Chimpanzees, gorillas, humans lemurs, monkeys, orangutans	165
Edentata	Most lack teeth	Anteaters, armadillos, sloths	30
Pholidota	Toothless mammals, body covered with scales	Pangolins	8
Lagomorpha	Short-tailed, gnawing mammals; two pairs of front teeth in upper jaw	Hares, rabbits, pikas	60

Order	General Description	Examples	Approximate Number of Species
Rodentia	Gnawing mammals; one pair of chisel-like front teeth in upper jaw, one pair in lower jaw	Beavers, gophers, mice, muskrats, porcupines, rats, squirrels, prairie dogs	1,690
Cetacea	Mammals that live in water and have paddle-like front limbs, no hind limbs, streamlined bodies and a breathing hole on top of head	Dolphins, porpoises, whales	85
Carnivora	Meat-eating mammals	Badgers, bears, cats, dogs, foxes, lions, otters, raccoons, skunks, tigers, weasels, wolves	285
Tubulidentata	Long-snouted, sticky-tongued mammals	Aardvarks	1
Proboscidea	Large, long-nosed (trunked) mammals	Elephants	2
Hyracoidea	Small rabbit-sized mammals	Hyraxes and dassies	11
Pinnipedia	Marine-based mammals with fur and fins	Seals, sea lions, walruses	31
Sirenia	Large, air-breathing ocean-dwelling mammals	Sea cows (manatees), dugongs	4
Perissodactyla	Odd-toed, hoofed mammals	Horses, rhinoceroses, tapirs, zebras	15
Artiodactyla	Even-toed, hoofed mammals	Antelopes, buffalo, camels, cows, deer, giraffes, goats, hippopotamuses, hogs, moose, sheep	170

Common Names and Scientific Names

All plants and animals have formal Latin names. Many also have common names, or nicknames. The formal name of a plant or animal is called the scientific name, and it is the same all over the world. A common name, however, can be different from place to place and in different languages.

Common names can sometimes be confusing because different kinds of plants or different kinds of animals may have the same common name. For example, if someone told you that they saw a trap-door spider, you could not be certain whether it was the spider that builds simple tube-like homes, the one that builds wishbone-shaped burrows, or the one that builds burrows with side doors.

In the table below, you will find the common name (nickname) and the scientific name (formal name) for each animal discussed in this book. Each scientific name has two parts.

The first part, called the genus, always begins with a capital letter. The genus includes the small group of animals that are similar to one another in many ways.

The second part of the scientific name, called the species, is not capitalized. The species includes animals that are exactly alike. If the exact species is not known, then the genus name is given alone.

Common Name	Scientific Name
Chimpanzee or chimp	*Pan troglodytes*
Gray squirrel or eastern gray squirrel	*Sciurus carolinensis*
Harvest mouse or European harvest mouse	*Micromys minutus*
European badger, Eurasian badger, or Old World badger	*Meles meles*
Prairie dog or black-tailed prairie dog	*Cynomys ludovicianus*
Common mole or Eastern mole	*Scalopus aquaticus*
Muskrat or musquash	*Ondatra zibethicus*
Beaver or American beaver	*Castor canadensis*

Glossary

brush Branches that have been broken off or cut off of trees; dense growth of bushes.

burrow A hole in the ground where an animal lives, hides, and raises its young.

camouflage (KAM-ah-flahj) Blending in with natural surroundings.

captivity The state of being kept confined, such as when an animal is kept in a cage.

carnivore A meat-eating animal.

chamber An enclosed space, such as a cave, room, or cell.

clan A group of families or individuals that come together because of a common interest.

class A large group of plants or animals that are alike in certain ways.

colony A group of animals of the same kind living together.

den The place an animal goes to rest, live, hide, or to raise its young.

diameter The length of a straight line that passes through the center of a circle or round object.

dray The leafy nest of a squirrel.

dung Animal excrement; manure.

foundation The base upon which something is built.

gland An organ in the body of an animal that stores and releases materials for use as needed. For example, your body's sweat glands release liquid onto your skin to help keep you cool.

habitat The place where a plant or animal normally lives, such as a desert, forest, or swamp.

insectivore (ihn-SEHK-tuh-vawr) An animal that feeds mainly on insects.

latrine (luh-TREEN) The dung pit used as a "bathroom" in an underground home.

life span The longest period of time that a particular animal can be expected to live in the wild or in captivity.

mammal A warm-blooded animal with a backbone whose young are fed with milk from special glands in the mother's body.

molehill A small mound of soil that has been pushed to the surface by a burrowing mole.

nursery A place where young are raised.

offspring The young of animals; descendants.

phylum (FY-luhm)(plural: phyla FY-LA) A large group of plants or animals; one of the primary divisions of the plant and animal kingdoms.

plunge hole shaft A secondary shaft

or emergency burrow entrance or exit; an entrance or exit to a beaver lodge.

prairie Flat or rolling land with tall grasses and few trees.

predator An animal that hunts, kills, and eats other animals.

prey (PRAY) An animal that is hunted, killed, and eaten by another animal.

primate A mammal with five toes on both its front and hind feet.

range The area in which a group of animals lives.

rodent Small, gnawing mammals, such as mice, squirrels, and beavers, that have a pair of chisel-like front teeth in both their upper and lower jaws; members of the order Rodentia.

run A shallow tunnel that a mole digs just below the surface of the ground.

scientific name The two-part Latin name given to every different kind, or species, of organism. Every species has its own scientific name; in this way, an organism has more than one common name can be properly identified worldwide.

sett (SEHT) The network of tunnels in which a badger lives.

species (SPEE-seez) A single category of organism which all share common characteristics.

suburb A neighborhood near a large city.

upstream The direction from which water comes in a stream; The opposite of downstream, the direction in which the water is flowing.

vegetation Plant life.

vertical In a straight, up-and-down position.

wedge To pack tightly or force something into a narrow space.

Source Notes

Banfield, A. W. F. *The Mammals of Canada*. Toronto, Canada: University of Toronto Press, 1981.

Bare, C. S. *Tree Squirrels*. New York: Dodd, Mead and Company, 1983.

Brady, Irene. *Beaver Year*. Boston: Houghton Mifflin, 1976.

Chace, G. Earl. *Wonders of Prairie Dogs*. New York: Dodd, Mead and Company, 1976.

Colby, C. B. *Wild Rodents*. New York: Meredith Press, 1967.

Corbet, G. B., and H. N. Southern. *The Handbook of British Mammals*. Oxford, England: Blackwell Scientific Publications, 1977.

Davis, Bette J. *Mole From the Meadow*. New York: Lothrop, Lee, and Shepard, 1970.

Goodall, Jane van Lawick. *In the Shadow of Man*. Boston: Houghton Mifflin, 1971.

Harris, Stephen. *The Harvest Mouse*. Dorset, England: Blandford Press, 1980.

Kinkead, Eugene. *Squirrel Book*. New York: E. P. Dutton, 1980.

Laycock, George. *Squirrels*. New York: Four Winds Press, 1975.

Long, Charles A., and Carl A. Killingley. *The Badgers of the World*. Springfield, Illinois: Charles C. Thomas Publishers, 1983.

———. *National Geographic Book of Mammals*. Vols. 1 and 2. Washington, D. C.: National Geographic Society, 1981.

Nowak, R. M., and J. L. Paradiso. *Walker's Mammals of the World*. Vols. 1 and 2. Baltimore: The Johns Hopkins University Press, 1983.

Oxford Scientific Films. *Grey Squirrel*. New York: G. P. Putnam's Sons, 1982.

———. *Harvest Mouse*. New York: G. P. Putnam's Sons, 1982.

Purkett, Molly. *The Year of the Badger*. Philadelphia: Lippincott, 1974.

Rue, L. Lee, III. *Pictorial Guide to the Mammals of North America*. New York: Thomas Y. Crowell, 1967.

Scheffel, Richard L., ed. *ABC's Of Nature*. New York: The Reader's Digest Association, Inc., 1984.

For More Information

Books

Fowler, Allan. *Animals Underground* (Rookie Read About Science). Danbury, CT: Children's Press, 1997.

Garcia, Eulalia. Gabriel Casadevall (Illustrator). *Moles: Champion Excavators* (Secrets in the Animal World). Milwaukee, WI: Gareth Stevens, 1997.

Miller, Sara Swan. *Rodents: From Mice to Muskrats* (Animals in Order). Danbury, CT: Franklin Watts, Inc., 1998.

Orr, Richard (Illustrator), Shaila Awan. *The Burrow Book*. New York, NY: DK
  Publishing, 1997.
Patent, Dorothy Hinshaw. William Munoz (Illustrator). *Prairie Dogs*. New York,
  NY: Clarion Books, 1993.

Videos
Mother Nature. *Good Neighbor Ground Squirrel*. 1993.
Mother Nature. *The Business of Beavers*. 1991.

Web Sites
The Badger's Sett
After viewing the picture gallery, find information on the classification of this
rodent, and badgers in the news—**www.thesett.freeserve.co.uk**.

The Squirrel Place
The history of the squirrel, including how it got its name, trivia, facts, links, and
some frequently asked squirrel questions—**www.squirrels.org**.

Index